ideals® HOME

More Than 50 Years of Celebrating Life's Most Treasured Moments

Vol. 53, No. 5

"Every house where love abides and friendship is a guest
Is surely home—and home, sweet home—
for there the heart can rest."

—Henry van Dyke

IDEALS—Vol. 53, No. 5 August MCMXCVI IDEALS (ISSN 0019-137X) is published eight times a year: February, March, May, June, August, September, November, December by IDEALS PUBLICATIONS INCORPORATED, 535 Metroplex Drive, Suite 250, Nashville, TN 37211. Second-class postage paid at Nashville, Tennessee, and additional mailing offices. Copyright © MCMXCVI by IDEALS PUBLICATIONS INCORPORATED. POSTMASTER: Send address changes to Ideals, PO Box 305300, Nashville, TN 37230. All rights reserved. Title IDEALS registered U.S. Patent Office.

SINGLE ISSUE—U.S. $5.95 USD; Higher in Canada
ONE-YEAR SUBSCRIPTION—8 issues—U.S. $19.95 USD; Canada $36.00 CDN (incl. GST and shipping); Foreign $25.95 USD
TWO-YEAR SUBSCRIPTION—16 issues—U.S. $35.95 USD; Canada $66.50 CDN (incl. GST and shipping); Foreign $47.95 USD

Printed and bound in USA by Quebecor Printing. Printed on Weyerhaeuser Husky.

The paper used in this publication meets the minimum requirements of
American National Standard for Information Sciences—
Permanence of Paper for Printed Library Materials, ANSI Z39.48-1984.

Subscribers may call customer service at 1-800-558-4343 to make address changes.
Unsolicited manuscripts will not be returned without a self-addressed, stamped envelope.

ISBN 0-8249-1138-5   GST 131903775

Cover Photo: COLONIAL PORCH.
Larry LeFever/Grant Heilman Photography, Inc.

Inside Front Cover: THE OLDEST HOUSE.
Walt Matthews, artist. Superstock.

Inside Back Cover: ARTILLERY LANE.
Walt Matthews, artist. Superstock.

Design for Living

Edna Jaques

A small place of your very own
Where every family lives alone
Beneath its sheltering maple trees,
Where you can do just as you please
Without a soul to tell you nay
Or cramp the children at their play.

A house with windows broad and wide
That seem to let in half outside,
A blue sky and a sun-crowned hill,
Beauty enough to almost fill
The very house with golden light,
And stars to shed their glow at night.

Wide bedrooms on an upper floor
With a clear view of lake and shore
Where ships are passing all day long,
A tree that holds a curlew's song
Cupped in its branches like a bar
Of music coming from afar.

A living room and fireplace
Where you can watch the fire and trace
The rings of growth in a tough knot,
A room where love and peace are caught
And held with careful hands lest they
Might lose their happiness some day.

Fashioned and made by loving toil
That naught of earth can change or spoil.

2

SUMMER RETREAT
Los Angeles, California
Mark Lohman/FPG International

Prayer for a New House

Edith Shaw Butler

Let this house shelter joy
    And dreams come true.
May someone love these rooms
    And keep them bright.
Let laughter and contentment
    Dwell here too
And children kneel to say
    Small prayers at night.
Perhaps there'll be
    A teakettle that sings
And scarlet blossoms
    On these windowsills;
A home is made
    Of just such little things.
Let someone love
    This view of distant hills.
Let firelight flicker
    On piano keys.
Let books and games
    And music have their part
And many, many shining
    Christmas trees
To warm the very cockles
    Of the heart.
Let such things weave
    A spell that will endear
This house to those
    So blessed as to live here.

OCEAN VIEW
Rockport, Massachusetts
Daniel Dempster Photography

Dream House

Catherine Parmenter Newell

Let there be within these phantom walls
Beauty where the hearth fire's shadow falls,
Quiet pictures, books, and welcoming chairs,
Music that the very silence shares,
Kitchen windows curtained blue and white,
Shelves and cupboards built for my delight,
Little things that lure and beckon me
With their tranquil joy! And let there be
Lilt of laughter, swift-forgotten tears
Woven through the fabric of the years,
Strength to guard me, eyes to answer mine,
Mutely clear. And though without may shine
Stars of dawn or sunset's wistful glow,
All of life and love my house shall know!

*"Our truest life
is when we are in
dreams awake."*

—Henry David Thoreau

Home, Sweet Home

Ruth E. McDaniel

A domicile, a habitat,
A place where you can hang your hat,
A residence where you can rest,
A small abode, a cozy nest,

A blazing hearth, an open door—
A home is all these things and more,
Where love and warmth and comfort dwell,
Where peace abides and all is well.

A sanctuary from the cold,
A house that beats with heart of gold,
A palace or a humble shack,
If it's your home it calls you back,

Back to the place where you belong.
You feel its pull; you hear its song.
There God's an ever-present guest;
Your home, sweet home—it's heaven-blessed.

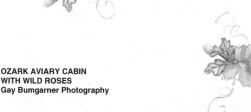

BITS & PIECES

*H*appy homes are built of blocks of patience.
—*Harold E. Kohn*

*S*weet is the smile of home, the mutual look
when hearts are of each other sure.
—*John Keble*

*W*hen in doubt, go home.
—*Author Unknown*

*Y*ou can no more measure a home by inches
or weigh it by ounces than you can set up
the boundaries of a summer breeze or calculate
the fragrance of a rose. Home is the love
which is in it.
—*Edward Whiting*

*H*ome—a place that our feet may leave,
but not our hearts.
—*Author Unknown*

$\mathcal{B}$ut what on earth is half so dear, so longed for,
as the hearth of home?

—*Emily Brontë*

$\mathcal{A}$ good laugh is sunshine in a house.

—*William Makepeace Thackeray*

$\mathcal{S}$trengthened by faith, these rafters will
Withstand the batt'ring of the storm;
This hearth, though all the world grow chill,
Will keep us warm.

—*Louis Untermeyer*

$\mathcal{S}$trength of character may be acquired at work,
but beauty of character is learned at home.
There the affections are trained. There the gentle
life reaches us.

—*Henry Drummond*

Small Town

Craig E. Sathoff

There's something 'bout the small town life
    That's friendship at its best,
For each and every warm "hello"
    Has extra special zest.

The soda fountain is a place
    Not just for ice-cream drinks
But to compare one's thoughts and views
    With what a neighbor thinks.

The bench outside the barbershop
    (The town directory)
Holds oldsters sitting neath the sun
    Who greet all cheerfully.

No man has cause to feel alone
    When trouble comes his way,
'Cause all the town will pitch right in
    To brighten up his day.

The pace of life moves ever slow,
    But no one can deny
That life is lived in fullest joy
    As days and years pass by.

"God gave us memories that we might have roses in December."

—Sir James M. Barrie

Home

Zenith Hess

I sometimes dream of a house I knew
Where perfumed roses adorned the view,
Where happy wren songs would often pour
From maple trees by the old back door.
With windows wide, 'twas no place for gloom
When sweet gales drifted from room to room;
And mem'ries filled every corner there
With children's laughter and joy to spare.
Each day was filled with a million things,
The work and play that a lifetime brings.

The Neighbor Lady
Who'll Buy Anything

Sally Nalbor

My doorbell sounds with that certain telltale ring; and by the kitchen clock, I see that school is out for the day. I peer down through the screen door and recognize the two neighbor girls standing on the front porch. Their little permed heads are cocked toward me; their large, hopeful eyes are fixed on mine. Maybe it's my imagination, but they seem to be quaking slightly in their bright pink anklets.

"Would you like to buy a Nutti-Choco candy bar?" one of them purrs as the other swings their box of wares upward for me to view. "It's for the girls' softball league," she adds softly.

"Well certainly," I reply without hesitation. "I could use some candy bars."

I take two bars, one per girl. While I rummage through my purse for my billfold, I try to engage them in conversation with anecdotes from my own glorious softball-playing days. I manage to elicit a few nods and several episodes of giggles.

As the two girls hop and skip down the drive, I hear one say matter-of-factly to the other, "See? I told you she'd buy some." The words greet me like old friends, and I wonder incredulously if I've become the neighbor lady who'll buy anything.

Surely every neighborhood has one. When I

was a child, ours was Mrs. Teegarden. She lived kitty-corner from my house in a sprawling, red brick ranch with big white double doors in front. Fittingly, her doorbell played "Happy Days Are Here Again." Mrs. Teegarden gave out large-sized candy bars on Halloween, always tipped the paperboy, and earned the reputation of being the neighbor lady who'd buy anything from a grade-schooler.

I'll never forget the expectant flush of confidence I felt as a child when I stood before those double doors and hummed in unison with the doorbell. I knew I could count on Mrs. Teegarden to buy a couple of boxes of Camp Fire Girl candy or a sheet or two of Christmas seals or whatever else I might be selling.

In fact, one summer day my best friend and I, apparently in desperate need of immediate funds, made a bright assortment of crayon shavings and packaged them in envelopes suitable (or so we thought) for sale. Not only did Mrs. Teegarden buy several packages, but she also invited us in for grape juice, which she served in crystal water goblets. Though my mother, aghast at our enterprise, made us return our crayon-shaving profits, Mrs. Teegarden was forever ensconced in my mind as the neighbor lady who'd buy anything.

Now, squeezing my newly acquired Nutti-Choco candy bars next to the others on the tightly packed cupboard shelf, I smile at the thought that I might indeed be an heir to the legacy of my dear neighbor. Oh, I don't pretend to possess the same mystique. My crystal goblets are packed away somewhere in the basement, and my doorbell is just a plain bingbonger. But when faced with a salesperson shorter than my doorknob, I can muster no more resistance than sweet Mrs. Teegarden.

As witness, my desk is awash with little league spaghetti dinner tickets and band booster coupon books. The refrigerator is stocked with crocks of swim team Cheddar cheese, boxes of cheerleader vanilla creams, and canned pound cakes, appropriately from the karate club. I have smiley-face potholders and a Frosty the Snowman candle I haven't the heart to light. Though it's doubtful I'll ever afford the Porsche that my husband jokingly asks for each Christmas, I do have enough wrapping paper to wrap it.

Every once in a while I vow to get tough and say no to all salespeople, regardless of their size or number of freckles. But just about that time, a rosy-cheeked Brownie scout will peek over my doorknob in her little felt beanie and melt my resolve like warm sunshine on a chocolate-mint cookie. As quick as you can sew on a merit badge, I'm rearranging the freezer once again to make room for a few more boxes of cookies.

Even near disasters don't discourage me. I recall the day I opened my door to a scrawny little boy, his blue eyes gazing up at me from behind oversized spectacles. He explained haltingly that he was participating in a swim-a-thon and needed sponsors to pledge a set amount of money for each lap he could swim the following Saturday at the city pool. He looked so fragile and small that I pledged a generous one dollar per lap. It wasn't until the next Sunday when he came to collect that I noticed his uncanny resemblance to a young Clark Kent. The child had swum twenty laps and, beaming broadly, informed me he would accept checks. Though I had to break out a few crocks of Cheddar cheese and thaw some boxes of cookies to stretch our food budget over the following weeks, I have never regretted my overzealous pledge.

Maybe my eagerness has something to do with how it felt to stand on Mrs. Teegarden's porch. Or perhaps it's how I feel now when a freckle-faced kid gives me a triumphant grin or a little voice says thank you with a new air of confidence. I realize there's a certain immeasurable pleasure in being the neighbor lady who'll buy anything.

My Neighbor Next Door

Kay Hoffman

A friendly path where roses climb
Leads from my neighbor's door to mine.
It brings my heart an added cheer
To know her friendship's ever near.

In wintertime when snow is deep,
An open pathway I must keep.
For should she need me, I must go.
My neighbor's old; her step is slow.

No fence divides her house and mine;
Our friendship needs no bound'ry line.
What's mine is hers; what's hers is mine,
A friendship proved by test of time!

Good neighbors living side by side.
If nations all would thus abide,
The wars would cease; life would be good,
Our world—a friendly neighborhood!

My Neighbor Friend

Clara Cline Thompson

I have a little neighbor friend
Who lives across the miles;
She never fails to welcome me
With lots of pleasant smiles.

She takes me to her garden green;
It is ablaze with bloom.
And when I'm feeling sad and low,
Her flowers chase the gloom.

There's always time for her to make
A cheery cup of tea
And test the rich, brown chocolate cake;
She says it's just for me.

She gives me bars of homemade soap,
A recipe for bread,
Then tells me not to make it yet
And gives a loaf instead.

But what she gives that's dearly prized,
The greatest gift of all,
Is filling me with friendship sweet
Whene'er I go to call.

TRAVELER'S Diary

Opal Simmons

Thursday morning, August
Cape May, New Jersey

We finally made it to Cape May yesterday. What a welcome the sunny, breezy weather was! East coast residents all of our lives, my husband and I have never before visited this lovely gem on the southern-most tip of New Jersey. How surprising to find this quiet Victorian village in a state so known for its cities and highways.

The brightly colored Victorian homes, complete with gingerbread decorations, charming cupolas, and shiny black wrought iron fences, kept our camera clicking all day. We met a local man who told us that the town was originally settled by Dutch whalers in the 1600s, but eventually its prime location on the Atlantic drew wealthy Americans looking for a resort spot. In the 1800s, our new friend told us, six American presidents took summer vacations here! I can understand the allure. Surrounded by water on three sides, Cape May is awash in refreshing ocean air.

Our day in Cape May was taken up by walks up and down the charming streets, lunch at a local inn, and shopping all afternoon. At dinner last night our innkeeper urged us to return in the fall to visit Cape May Point, just two miles west. Every autumn millions of birds, including hawks, owls, swallows, warblers, ducks, geese, and shorebirds, stop at Cape May Point on their way to their winter homes. We promised to return to Cape May without hesitation; like so many before us, we have been taken under its spell.

GINGERBREAD DREAMS
Cape May, New Jersey
Peter Gridley/FPG International

My Little House and Me

John C. Bonser

You'd pass my house a thousand times
    And not heed it at all.
The lawn's just fair and somewhat bare;
    The rooms are kind of small.

A window's cracked, some paint has peeled,
    The aging floorboards creak;
My house is not historical
    Or even just unique.

The furniture is rather worn;
    I've nothing really new.
And yet this house belongs to me,
    And I will make it do.

It is a comfort just to know
    As I walk down life's lane,
My house is there to shelter me
    From cold and wind and rain.

You'd pass by me a hundred times
    In stores or shopping mall
And never take a second look
    Or notice me at all.

I'm certainly no fashion plate;
    My clothes are neat but plain.
I show no signs of worldly wealth
    Or temporary gain.

And still, just like this house of mine,
    I've much that I could share,
A kindly warmth that glows inside,
    A willingness to care.

But many, many pass us by
    And never really see
How much worthwhile dwells here within
    My little house and me!

THROUGH MY WINDOW

Pamela Kennedy

Art by Russ Flint

POLITICS BEGIN AT HOME

While I'm just as patriotic as the next person, I don't consider myself particularly politically minded. We lived in Washington, D.C., for three years, and I enjoyed visiting the Capitol and watching the congressmen and women make their speeches; but I have never been involved passionately in a campaign or cause. I have, however, noted with interest the increase in women's forums, conferences, and so forth; and I am becoming convinced that there is a large group of women who are seriously under-represented at such meetings. When these conferences end and the final draft of demands is published, I never read about the urgency to implement the kinds of rights I would personally enjoy.

Because of this void on our political land-scape, and despite my inexperience in the political realm, I decided to call together a caucus in my living room with my fellow homemakers. It was time to stand up and be counted. After all, we are women who have faced life on the battle lines and in the car-pool lines; we have fed the starving adolescent masses who are yearning to be free. No longer are we willing to merely take a back seat in the minivan of life, to serve from the stove and never have a place at the table. We have determined to make our demands known and are choosing this forum to debut our Homemaker's Manifesto!

HOMEMAKER'S MANIFESTO

1. We want the right to soak in a bubble bath without having anyone barge into the bathroom asking questions that "can't wait"—especially if that person brings along two or three friends!

2. We want the right to tell our side of the story without being interrupted with petty inquiries about details or requests to "just get to the bottom line."

3. We think we deserve the right to dent a fender now and then and not have to face an inquisition.

4. Once in a while we would appreciate the right to lie down in the afternoon and not have others assume we must be sick or near death.

5. We reserve the right to ask "mother questions," such as:
    a. Where do you think you are going dressed like that?
    b. Do you believe money grows on trees?
    c. And just when were you planning to tell me about this?
    d. You think you're sorry *now?*

6. We want the right to watch a television program from start to finish without someone hitting the remote control just when the plot gets interesting.

7. When traveling, we desire the right to stop at antique shops and garage sales and vegetable stands without prior planning.

8. We want to be able to read meaningless fluff and not be asked to explain "why anyone would spend time on such drivel."

9. With respect to our culinary rights, we request the opportunity to make a new casserole recipe without divulging all the ingredients before anyone will taste it.

10. We want the right to hug our teen-agers in public.

It was difficult to hammer out this manifesto; but by the time the second pot of coffee and the bar cookies were depleted, we had narrowed our demands to these ten. We agreed it was at least a starting place and acknowledged that all great causes probably trace their histories to just such small beginnings. After pledging our allegiance to one another and to our determination to make things better for homemakers everywhere, we adjourned our meeting.

You know, I just had no idea that the political process could be so exciting and invigorating! I could have gone on for hours and hours; but it was Tuesday, which means the afternoon car-pool, and then baseball practice and piano lessons. And I still had to pick up the dry-cleaning, return overdue library books, and get home in time to disguise the mushrooms in the lasagna. I wonder if this is how a congresswoman feels?

Pamela Kennedy is a freelance writer of short stories, articles, essays, and children's books. Wife of a naval officer and mother of three children, she has made her home on both U.S. coasts and currently resides in Honolulu, Hawaii. She draws her material from her own experiences and memories, adding highlights from her imagination to enhance the story.

The Low, Green Hills of Home

J. Harold Gwynne

Once more with eager, raptured eyes,
With quickened pulse and heart that thrills,
I gaze upon my native home
At rest among the circling hills.

Wherever life may lead me on,
However far I chance to roam,
I long to see those sheltering hills
That were the low, green hills of home.

Those hills were once the distant rim
Of all the world my boyhood knew.
I lived and moved within their walls
And never dreamed of larger view.

As venturing boys we roamed those hills
On many bold and thrilling quests;
Our lively fancies led us on
From deepest vales to highest crests.

As cowboys, pirates, hunters, knights,
We bravely rode and fought and bled;
The rocks and caves, the streams and woods
Re-echoed oft our valiant tread.

All quiet now those peaceful scenes
And free from running, trampling feet;
The boys are gone; the games are done;
Gone are the yesterdays so sweet.

But when I stand in silence now,
Beside some old, familiar spot,
With vivid sense I live again
The early days long since forgot.

When sunset colors softly blend
Around those hills verdant and low,
The fading scene sinks in my heart
To cheer me on where'er I go.

SANTA LUCIA RANGE
San Luis Obispo County, California
Jeff Gnass Photography

An Old Homeplace

Virginia Borman Grimmer

Now one can travel miles on end,
Discover wonders at road's bend;
But nothing on this good earth's face
Can charm quite like an old homeplace,

A house where laughter rang in halls
And Mother's bell pealed dinner calls.
The fresh-washed linens hung outdoors,
And folks were happy with their chores.

The home-baked cookies, bread in loaves—
All came with loving hands from stoves.
Quaint crocheted doilies, tatted lace—
All added to the old homeplace.

The cellar room held put-up wares
Like applesauce and golden pears;
At least five hundred quarts it held
Beside black walnuts freshly shelled.

Oh, cities have their own allure
And modern houses fun to tour;
But in one's memory road to trace
There's nothing like an old homeplace.

Buying a Farm

Rose Koralewsky

You've bought a farm? Where? . . .
Oh, I know that place!
An ancient pine, some cedars, a small brook;
A hilly bit (thistles and goldenrod);
A patch of hardhack, a few barberries;
An old stone wall—you see, I know it well.
When winter sunsets blazed behind that pine
And all the western sky was molten gold,
I've stood there watching until darkness fell.
In spring I've seen the little brook go mad,
Foaming and gurgling while the tall, young trees
Stepped timidly along its margin green.
The summer's heat I've oft forgotten there
While resting in a pool of breezy shade
And listening to a distant tanager.
Just now, I know there's goldenrod in bloom,
Tall purple thistles, gay red barberries.
Then later, when the leaves begin to turn . . .
And you have bought all this? . . .
The deed? . . . I see . . .
The title's yours. The rest belongs to me.

GRANDPA'S FARM
Vermont
Ron Thomas/FPG International

A SLICE OF LIFE

Edgar A. Guest

HOME AND CHILDREN

My father often used to say
    When children he'd discuss,
"If ours are happier away,
    There's something wrong with us.
I'd think it shame my lifetime through
    If this should ever be—
They'd rather eat a neighbor's food
    Than stay with us for tea."

My father wasn't social wise;
    Grave books he'd never read.
He thought the mother should be home
    To see her babies fed.
"It is a lifetime job," said he,
    "That parents all assume.
I'd rather keep the children's love,
    Than keep a tidy room.

"I'd hate to think the neighbors gave
    What often we deny;
Our cookies kept on topmost shelves
    And theirs left handy by.
I'd think it shame if down the street
    Lived gentler folks than we,
Who made of home a happy place
    Where children liked to be.

"So have the cookies near at hand
    And give these rooms to fun.
Let children all be happy here
    Until the day is done.
Let's keep this home with joy aglow
    And free from fret and fuss;
For should they rather elsewhere be
    The fault would lie with us."

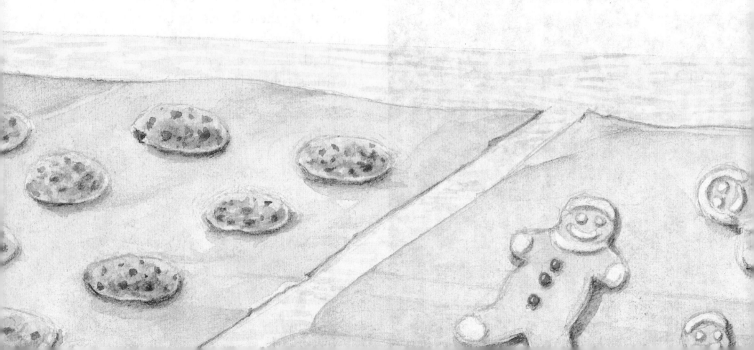

Edgar A. Guest began his illustrious career in 1895 at the age of fourteen when his work first appeared in the Detroit Free Press. His column was syndicated in over 300 newspapers, and he became known as "The Poet of the People."

Patrick McRae is an artist who lives in the Milwaukee, Wisconsin, area. He has created nostalgic artwork for Ideals for more than a decade, and his favorite models are his wife and three children.

Tabby

Victoria H. B. Widry

I cannot catch
This undirected, wispy,
Fleeting
Ball of running fur
Who streaks across
My polished floor
And disappears
Before my very eyes
Like flashes

In a humid summer night.
Then when he's had enough
Happy play,
He leaps
Onto his favorite chair
And curls into a downy ball,
Emitting contented purrs,
Then melts into
His treasured sleep.

34

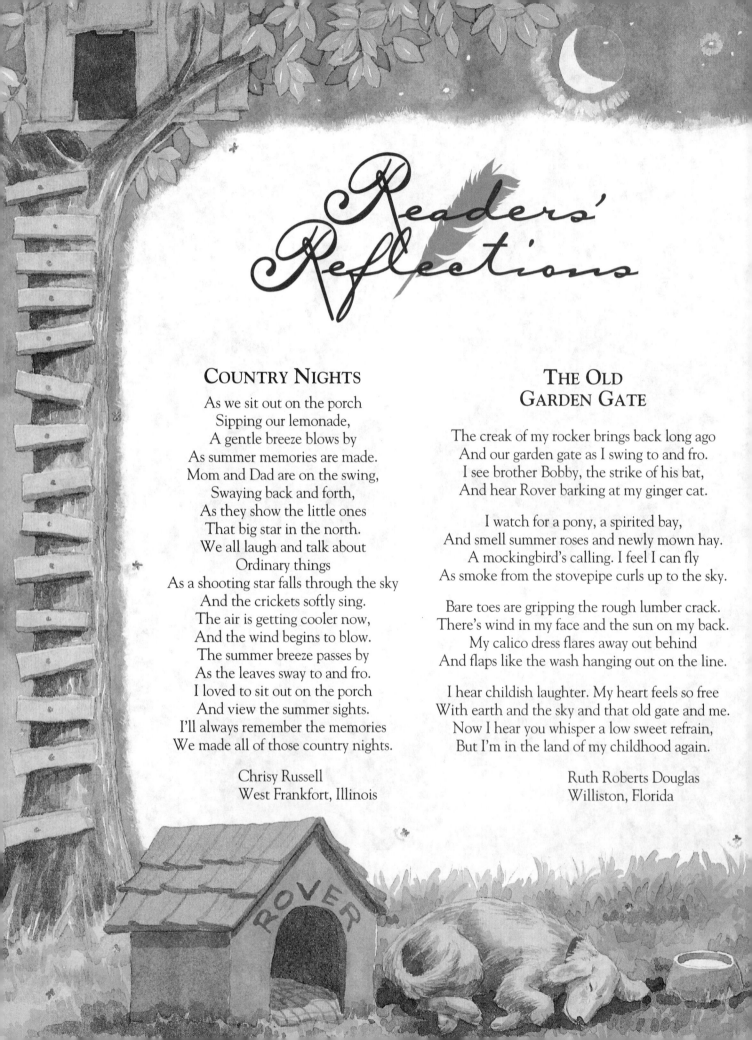

Readers' Reflections

COUNTRY NIGHTS

As we sit out on the porch
Sipping our lemonade,
A gentle breeze blows by
As summer memories are made.
Mom and Dad are on the swing,
Swaying back and forth,
As they show the little ones
That big star in the north.
We all laugh and talk about
Ordinary things
As a shooting star falls through the sky
And the crickets softly sing.
The air is getting cooler now,
And the wind begins to blow.
The summer breeze passes by
As the leaves sway to and fro.
I loved to sit out on the porch
And view the summer sights.
I'll always remember the memories
We made all of those country nights.

Chrisy Russell
West Frankfort, Illinois

THE OLD GARDEN GATE

The creak of my rocker brings back long ago
And our garden gate as I swing to and fro.
I see brother Bobby, the strike of his bat,
And hear Rover barking at my ginger cat.

I watch for a pony, a spirited bay,
And smell summer roses and newly mown hay.
A mockingbird's calling. I feel I can fly
As smoke from the stovepipe curls up to the sky.

Bare toes are gripping the rough lumber crack.
There's wind in my face and the sun on my back.
My calico dress flares away out behind
And flaps like the wash hanging out on the line.

I hear childish laughter. My heart feels so free
With earth and the sky and that old gate and me.
Now I hear you whisper a low sweet refrain,
But I'm in the land of my childhood again.

Ruth Roberts Douglas
Williston, Florida

SUMMER SOUNDS

Have you ever listened
On a hot summer night
To the sounds you can hear
As the moon shines bright?

I raise up the window
And turn on the fan.
The crickets are singing
As loud as they can.

The chirping of birds
Makes a song full of glee
As they perch in their nest
At the top of the tree.

As the curtains blow open,
I feel the warm breeze.
When listening I hear
Loud rustling of leaves.

Way in the distance,
I see a light flash.
As the storm moves closer,
I can hear thunder crash.

For just a short while,
The rain pours down.
After such a hot day,
It cools off the ground.

As I lay down to rest
After a long summer day,
The sounds are now quiet
And have nothing to say.

Debbie Bise
Glade Spring, Virginia

THE TREE HOUSE

In memory I still see it there,
The tree house high in summer air,
Scrap wood, foot holders carefully laid
Against the truck toward the stockade.

Two little boys with nails and hammer,
Arm loads of wood, and up they clamber,
Lifting wood pieces against mulberry bark,
Then climbing the tree to make a mark
Where their house floor will rest secure
On three huge limbs that shall endure.

The tree is tall; the limbs stretch long;
The nailed-down floor is very strong.
More wood is raised to build each side
For the fortress where they will hide.
Once floor and walls are all in place,
The tree house has enormous space,
Enough room for their friends to share,
As well as toys and favorite chair.

Rigging a pulley with heavy rope,
They lift provisions, as well as hope
That they may remain there near the sky,
To explore, to dream, and let time pass by.

Jessie Swihart
Houston, Texas

Ride the Wind Vane Horse

Lon Myruski

Atop our red barn roof he tends
    His weathered, tin terrain;
A caracoling copper steed
    With tarnished hocks and mane.
Old friend of farm and family,
    Of birds who flock in scores
To perch upon his proud, taut back
    And ride the wind vane horse.

He sallies from the morning mist
    To meet his barnyard friends,
Delighting in their lows and moos
    All day, till dusk descends.

Then come the tuneful katydids,
    Sweet midnight troubadours,
As Mr. Moon beams o'er the barn
    To ride the wind vane horse.

He gallops on neath gathering clouds
    To rhythmic country winds,
Line dancing to a banjo breeze
    With raindrop mandolins.
And from my bed in dreams I watch
    His wonderful encores;
Adrift on childhood reveries,
    I ride the wind vane horse.

CIRCUS EQUESTRIENNE, c. 1885
Shelburne Museum, Shelburne, Vermont
Photograph by Ken Burris

FOR THE CHILDREN
ARTWORK BY RUSS FLINT

SONG FOR A LITTLE HOUSE
Christopher Morley

I'm glad our house is a little house,
Not too tall nor too wide;
I'm glad the hovering butterflies
Feel free to come inside.

Our little house is a friendly house,
It is not shy or vain;
It gossips with the talking trees
And makes friends with the rain,

And quick leaves cast a shimmer of green
Against our whited walls,
And in the phlox the courteous bees
Are paying duty calls.

The unique perspective of Russ Flint's artistic style has made him a favorite of Ideals *readers for many years. A resident of California and father of four, Russ Flint has illustrated a children's Bible and many other books.*

The Family

Donna R. Lydston

So blessed are they who round a family board
May gather. May they humbly thank the Lord,
Not only for the food they common share,
But for the dear, loved faces circled there.
So oft, unless we face that board alone,
We treasure not its true, sweet sense of home.

So blessed are they, when low the pale stars ride,
If cheer, and warmth, and welcome safe abide
Within their shelter. Patient they would grow,
Kinder, more understanding, could they know
How empty is the house where no glad light
Shines from its windows out upon the night.

So blessed are they who have within their home
That touch of kinship, folks they call their own,
Flesh of their flesh. Ah, how they'd earnest strive
To ease small tensions, keeping love alive,
If once they knew the desolate despair
That haunts the house with no one waiting there.

CORNER

THIMBLES

by May Bradstreet

COLLECTOR'S

Browsing through a dusty antique shop on a rainy day several summers ago, I paused when my eye caught two small, glass display cases among the bric-a-brac. Each case held a dozen collectible thimbles, some porcelain white and painted with birds and flowers, others of carefully molded pewter or silver. I couldn't help but smile as I remembered another rainy Saturday when as a young girl my mother patiently showed me how to thread a needle and push it through the fabric that I held tightly between my fingers. After I received a few sharp pricks from the misguided needle, Mother offered her thimble, which teetered about on my small finger like an oversized metal hat. My fingers were saved, and I went on to learn to sew, though never quite as deftly as Mother.

Perhaps those memories of drizzly afternoons spent at my mother's side made me appreciate these simple, bell-shaped tools that have protected the fingers of countless needleworkers over the years. It's no surprise that my appreciation, fueled by the endearing charm and many delightful designs of the thimble, grew into my own thimble collection.

I now have shining glass display cases in my home to hold my treasured assortment of gold, silver, brass, and china thimbles. Each thimble has its own special features that first drew me to it.

My prized addition was a thimble discovered at the bottom of an old, cluttered sewing basket I bought at an auction. Underneath the jumbled pile of faded thread and knitting needles, I uncovered a gold thimble sporting a wide crescent border of forget-me-nots and the engraved name "Martha." I often find myself wondering what Martha and the other past owners of my thimbles were like and what heartfelt projects were stitched with the help of each small thimble.

Although I hold every thimble in my collection quite dear, my favorite piece has always been a tiny, childsize, pewter thimble adorned with a simple grapevine. Soon, the miniature bell will fit snugly on the dainty fingertip of my young daughter, and I will patiently teach her to stitch her name on a piece of cloth. I'm just waiting for the perfect rainy Saturday.

ANTIQUE THIMBLES WITH THREAD. Shelburne Museum, Shelburne, Vermont. Photograph by Ken Burris.

R. Blackinton & Co.   Thomas S. Brogan   D. C. Bourquin   S. Cottle Co.   Crane & Thevrer   Joseph F. Chatellier

JUST A THIMBLEFUL

If you would like to start a thimble collection of your own, here are some facts you will want to know:

HISTORY

- Ancient thimbles discovered among ruins of Pompeii, dating before A.D. 79.
- Word may have derived from *thumb-bell* because first worn on the thumb.
- Modern thimble designed in 1684 by Nicholas Van Benscholen of Amsterdam.
- Different materials, styles, and patterns reflect periods of design in metalsmithing.
- Made by many early-American silversmiths, including Paul Revere.

FREQUENT DESIGNS

Borders
- Crests and scrollwork
- Animals and birds
- Romantic symbols such as hearts, stars, and cherubs
- Symbols of prosperity such as flowers and fruits

Styles
- Handpainted with landscapes or scenes
- Adorned with inset jewels or stones such as coral, turquoise, amethyst, and jade
- Covered in delicate silver wire filigree

Markings
- Patent date or trademark (as shown above)
- Touchmark of the metalsmith
- Owner's monogram, name, or motto
- Message from gift-giver

THIMBLE MATERIALS

- gold
- silver
- onyx
- brass
- copper
- pewter
- bone
- ivory
- glass
- porcelain
- bone china
- jade
- leather
- colored silk
- wood
- tortoiseshell
- aluminum
- steel
- rubber
- plastic
- enamel
- pinchbeck

INTERESTING PIECES

- Souvenir thimbles from a specific location or vacation spot
- Commemorative thimbles specially commissioned in celebration of a noteworthy event
- Tailors' thimbles with open tops
- Tiny children's thimbles inscribed with nursery rhymes
- Plastic thimbles used to advertise businesses or political campaigns
- Novelty thimbles with attached threadcutters, needle threaders, magnets to attract the needle, or slots to protect long fingernails
- Made-to-order thimbles from the turn of the century that were set with diamonds
- Custom-made thimble cases or holders to protect fine thimbles
- Collapsible thimbles with separate parts which fit into one another like an old-fashioned drinking cup

Reminders

Evelynn Merilatt Boal

I keep her silver thimble
   In a little wooden box;
Beside it lies the walnut ball
   She used when darning socks.
And in a drawer, some pillowslips—
   Embroidered and crocheted
With flowers and dainty edgings—
   Join other things she made.

With love she planned each pattern;
   With care, each flower traced.
Her finger wore this thimble;
   Her hands the stitches placed.
Her handiwork is worn now,
   But oh, so dear to me.
I touch these things and feel her close—
   A breath of memory.

MOTHER'S ROOM
Blackfan
H. Armstrong Roberts

HANDMADE HEIRLOOM

WHITE WORK PLACE MAT. Embroidered by Mary Skarmeas. Jerry Koser Photography.

WHITE WORK PLACE MAT

Mary Skarmeas

My dear aunt Esther lives in one of those wonderful old Victorian homes filled with worn but cherished, antique furniture, an astonishing assortment of cuckoo clocks, and a pampered poodle named Elizabeth. Crocheted doilies and other such dainty things cover most every available surface throughout her home. While setting the table for an early dinner with Aunt Esther last Saturday, I went to the sideboard for linen napkins and spied a set of creamy white place mats with intricate white embroidery. Despite the age of the linens, the embroidery verily gleamed in the sunlight streaming through the tall windows. Aunt Esther explained that they were white work table linens given to her by a long-ago neighbor. So piqued was my creative spirit that I decided to put down my knitting needles and resurrect my embroi-

dery hoop in order to add a special touch of white to my own set of place mats.

White work is needlework done in white thread on a white fabric, but this simple definition belies the true beauty of the craft. Because of the basic simplicity of white on white, the stitches must have a pristine, even smoothness that blends perfectly with the fabric. The impeccable stitches enhance the texture of the fabric as well as the clarity of the embroidered design.

Like most of the handcrafts that we so enjoy today, white work has a long and varied history. Because of the easy adaptability of fabrics and threads, the cultural preferences of textures and designs, and the interchange of stitches and styles, the exact progress of any one particular type of white work has been difficult to follow. Throughout

48

history, women and girls of all ages were expected to become adept at embroidery. No matter what the social class, it was part of their education. For those of the lower class, embroidery was a skill valued for employment; domestics who were skillful with a needle had an easier life than those in the scullery.

For the upper classes, who had idle hours to fill, embroidery was a source of creativity and personal satisfaction. Great ladies of the nobility, as well as nuns, served their churches by embroidering the beautiful altar linens and the clergymen's garments.

The oldest known example of white work embroidery is a type of hairnet that was unearthed from a three-thousand-year-old grave in Denmark. Other pieces of white work have appeared in many countries and in many forms all over the world. White work seems to have originated in the East, most likely China, and then progressed to France and England before making its way to America.

Without knowing it, we have probably seen some examples of white work on white muslin clothing made in India or Pakistan. Tourists visiting the Philippines often bring home delicately embroidered white-on-white shirts and women's handbags made with a finely woven, sheer pineapple cloth called *piña* that is indigenous to that country.

White work crafts evoke images of the bygone days of embroidered collars and frilly bonnets. The Victorians especially loved white work and decorated nearly everything made of white fabric with white thread. Although it began with a few simple stitches, it soon became more complex and competitive. During the Victorian period in America, young girls were taught to embroider simple white stitches on handkerchiefs. Collars and cuffs were embroidered with the popular feather stitch; and many patient hands turned christening gowns into exquisite, one-of-a-kind heirlooms by adding the elegant texture of satin stitches and French knots.

With a few simple supplies, you can create your own uniquely personal piece of white work. Before you head to the craft store to find supplies for your own heirloom, however, consider your choices carefully. The beauty of white work is determined by the various textural qualities of the fabric, thread, and stitches you choose. Because of the influx of synthetics, many of the original fabrics used in white work are difficult to find; and some are no longer available at all. Luckily we have seen a return of

natural fibers; and although we may not find French muslin, Indian mull, or longcloth, you will be able to find organdy, batiste, Indian cotton, and linen. As for the embroidery floss, most craft stores carry a good quality, six-strand cotton. After you choose your fabric and thread, you will need needles to correspond to the size of the thread and a hoop or a frame—hand-held hoops for small pieces and standing frames for large projects.

It matters not what item you choose to embroider; the dramatic simplicity and beauty of white on white will show off your needle skill to its best advantage. Any embroidery pattern you desire can be transferred to your choice of fabric, but be sure that you use a washable blue marker or blue carbon as it seems to be the only color that will wash out of most fabrics and will also blend into the white thread. Always test your fabric first.

If the fabric you choose is thin enough to see through, as was the batiste that I chose for the place mat I embroidered, you can place it over the design and carefully secure it and trace it. If the fabric is heavy, first trace the design onto tissue or tracing paper and then transfer it to the fabric with carbon paper. From then on, the technique is pretty much the same whether you are an advanced needleworker or a beginner. Each clean and careful stitch will slowly bring your design to life.

Everything about white work embroidery lends itself to the creation of a lovely heirloom piece. From the choice of fabric, which can be the sheerest stark-white organdy or a creamy off-white fine wool, to the many varieties of thread, such as cotton, silk pearl twisted cotton, Japanese silk, silk ribbon thread, or white crewel yarn, the opportunity to create something unique and of lasting quality is guaranteed. While Aunt Esther was impressed with my careful stitches and the charming design on my place mats, she confessed that she preferred her own set, aged though they were. I can only hope that some future heir of mine will cherish my embroidery as much and feel a connection through time to a long-ago fellow lover of beautiful things.

Mary Skarmeas lives in Danvers, Massachusetts, and has recently earned her bachelor's degree in English at Suffolk University. Mother of four and grandmother of two, Mary loves all crafts, especially knitting.

Grandma's Legacy

Shannon Dyer

W arm and rich it dribbles from the spoon, and I think again that surely this is the perfection after which countless cooks have sought. At once it is fragile and delicate, yet thick and sturdy. Comprised of ordinary, everyday ingredients, its simplicity belies its magical taste. One spoonful holds the history of family tradition. My grandma's butter sauce—one cup sugar, one stick butter, three-fourths cup cream, a dash of salt. What could be easier? Put all of the ingredients in a saucepan, cook over medium heat for ten minutes, and you have a small taste of heaven, a real gourmet treat. The apple cake that it is poured over serves merely as a stage for this mouth-watering delicacy.

I stand at the stove and stir the mystical concoction. When my daughters aren't looking, I dip my fingers in and steal a taste, an action so uncouth that I'd never tolerate it from them. Though everyone to whom I've served the butter sauce loves it, my own love for it isn't just about taste, it's about my grandma. I guess I was always too busy to notice it when I was growing up. Maybe I was out the door before dessert was served; but whatever the reason, I don't remember

something different like stewed prunes. I was a picky eater and didn't like everything; Grandma's lunches were so unlike the suburban fare I knew at home. I was always skeptical of tasting the canned fruit that she brought up from the basement because it didn't come from big metal cans with fancy labels; instead it swam in glass quart jars with two-piece lids. Grandma made a great pimiento cheese spread; I used to love to watch in amazement as the soft cheese went through her ancient meat grinder. And I remember the airy cream puffs she filled with her own special, whipped-cream concoction—delicious.

But it's the butter sauce that brings my grandmother to my heart. I am connected to Grandma and to our noble line of ancestors that stretches back for generations—strong women, pioneers, groundbreakers. I am proud to be carrying their genes. Sometimes I think they're walking with me, daring me to step up and claim my place in the world. This pride in my heritage was handed down to me, like the butter sauce, from Grandma.

I remember one summer afternoon in particular. I sat down on her living room floor to help her sort through a "family box" of pictures, documents, and newspaper clippings. As I looked through the mementoes, I realized that those women before me had real lives full of their own challenges, triumphs, and heartbreaks. I saw the wise and calm gray-haired woman who sat in her recliner in the avocado green living room as a spirited young wife and, before that, a mischievous girl. She's a link in the chain, just like me. Grandma has been the keeper of the family for three generations; and that day, she passed the keepsakes—and the stories—down to me. She guarded our history, and she gave me the gift and responsibility to carry on the continuity of the ages.

So I'll continue to make the butter sauce and pour it over the basic apple cake. As I watch my little girls smack their lips after each golden spoonful, I know I am giving them much more than a simple, sweet treat. I am passing along the torch of our family's heritage. My grandma's blood flows in their veins too, and that's a legacy to be proud of.

eating it in her kitchen. The butter sauce, like Grandma, I came to appreciate much later.

Its taste reminds me of Grandma, all warm and sweet and uncomplicated. There's no trick to making the sauce, no secret, no special rule. Dump everything in a pan, heat, and stir. But you have to use real ingredients; margarine won't work, and don't even think about using skim milk or artificial sweetener. I've never ruined it; I don't think a person could, unless it were neglected or scorched.

Most of my childhood memories of Grandma center around the kitchen. Lunch at Grandma's house always consisted of interesting leftovers—

Ideals' Family Recipes

Favorite Recipes from the Ideals Family of Readers

Editor's Note: Please send us your best-loved recipes! Mail a typed copy of the recipe along with your name, address, and phone number to Ideals magazine, ATTN: Recipes, P.O. Box 305300, Nashville, Tennessee 37230. We will pay $10 for each recipe used. Recipes cannot be returned.

BUFFET GREEN BEANS

In a large skillet, place 8 slices of bacon, chopped, and 1 large sliced onion. Fry over medium heat until bacon is crisp. Remove from skillet and drain on paper towels, reserving ¼ cup drippings in skillet.

In a small bowl, mix together ½ cup white vinegar and ¼ cup granulated sugar. Pour mixture into skillet with reserved drippings and bring to a boil. Add three 14½-ounce cans of drained, cut, green Italian beans. Cook over medium heat until blended, stirring occasionally. Spoon into serving dish with a slotted spoon and top with crumbled bacon and onion. Makes 8 servings.

Mrs. John B. Wright
Greenville, South Carolina

TOMATO SALAD

In a large bowl, mix together 8 chopped, fresh tomatoes, ½ cup chopped onions, ½ cup chopped celery, and 1 chopped green pepper; set aside. In a small bowl, combine ½ cup white vinegar, ½ cup granulated sugar, and salt to taste. Pour vinegar mixture over vegetables; stir to coat. Refrigerate until serving. Makes 8 servings.

Mrs. Donald Rogers
Le Roy, Kansas

BAKED SUMMER SQUASH

Preheat oven to 350° F. In a greased baking dish, place 3 cups summer squash cut into strips. Cover squash with ¼ cup milk, and dot with 2 tablespoons butter or margarine. Sprinkle with 1 teaspoon salt, ¼ teaspoon paprika, and 1 teaspoon fresh lemon thyme. Cover and bake 30 minutes or until tender. Before serving, garnish with crisp, crumbled bacon. Makes 4 servings.

Kay Prater
Clovis, New Mexico

KINGLY SKILLET CABBAGE

In a large skillet, heat 1 tablespoon olive oil over low heat. Add 1 cup chopped green pepper, 5 cups chopped cabbage, and 3 chopped garlic cloves. Sauté 10 minutes. Stir in ½ cup water, ¼ teaspoon salt, and 1 tablespoon chopped, fresh rosemary. Cover and simmer for about 25 minutes, stirring occasionally. Add 1 cup sliced, fresh mushrooms. Simmer uncovered 3 to 5 minutes. Sprinkle with ⅛ teaspoon black pepper and serve warm with cornbread muffins. Makes 4 to 6 servings.

Ms. Jimmie Fleming
Chester, Virginia

FANCY VIDALIA ONIONS AU GRATIN

Preheat oven to 350° F. Slice approximately 2 Vidalia onions into thin rings to fill 3 cups. In a medium skillet over medium heat, sauté onions with 2 tablespoons butter or margarine until soft but not browned.

In a separate bowl, mix together ½ cup self-rising flour, 2 tablespoons butter or margarine, 1 beaten egg, 2 cups grated Cheddar or Swiss cheese, and a dash of salt and pepper. Add to onions and mix well. Cook over medium heat until butter and cheese are melted and mixture is no longer sticky. Pour mixture into a buttered casserole and top with an additional ½ cup grated cheese. Bake 20 to 30 minutes. Makes approximately 6 servings.

Doris S. Aldridge
Decatur, Alabama

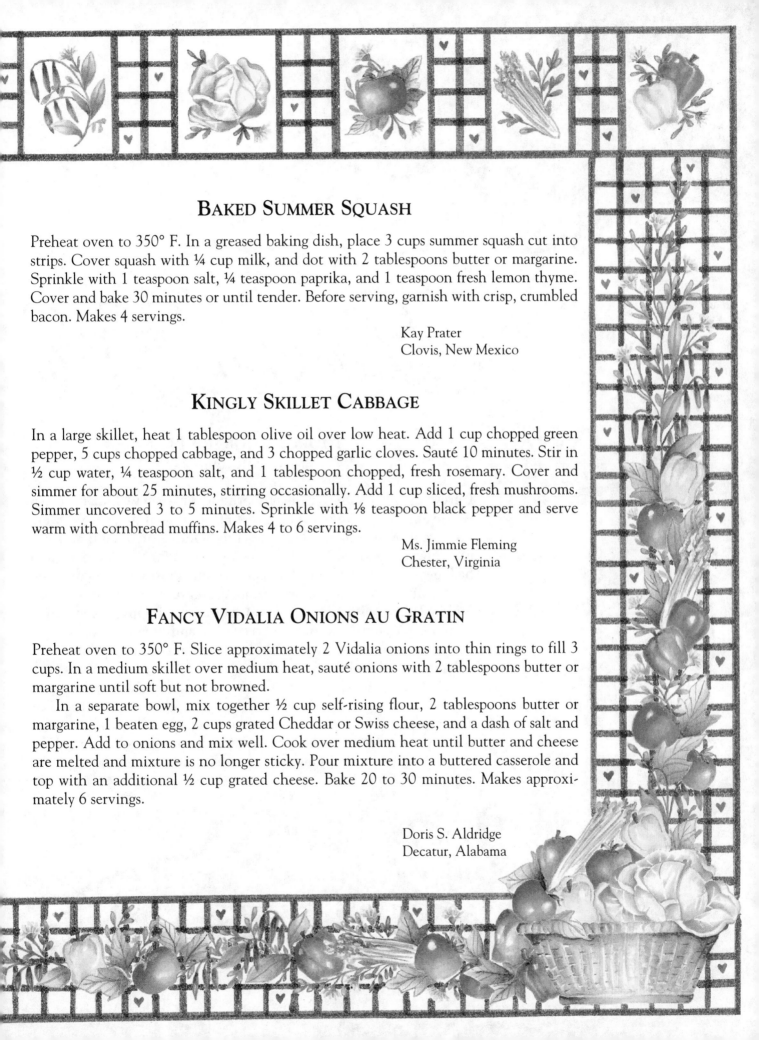

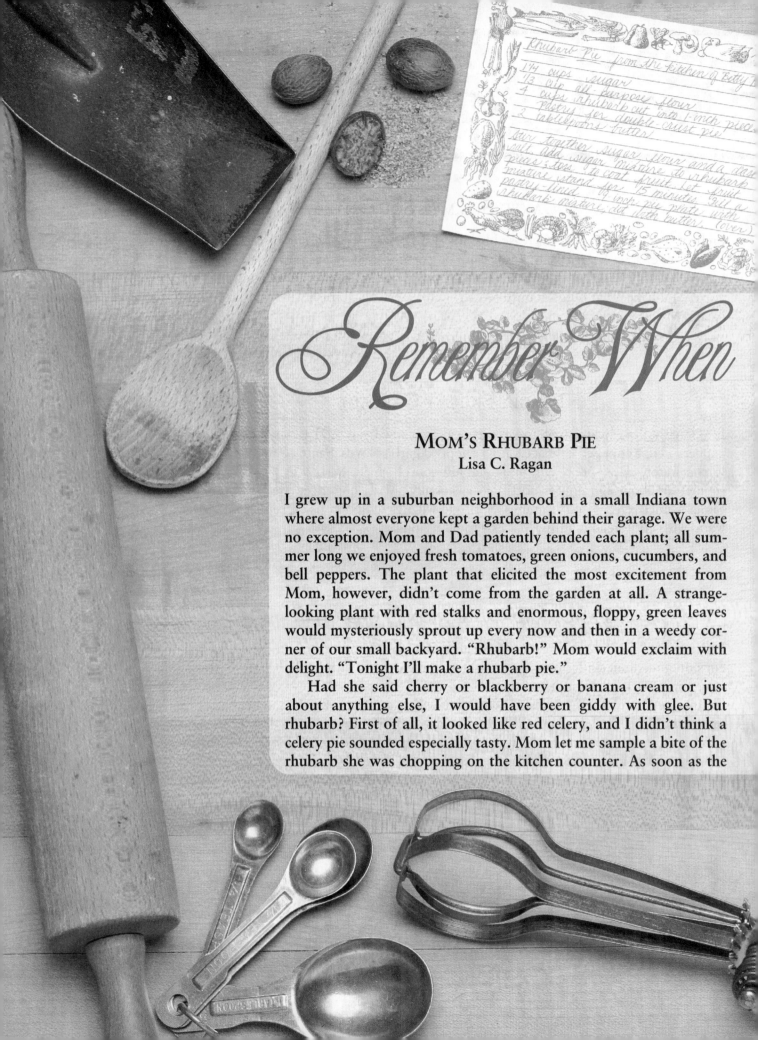

MOM'S RHUBARB PIE
Lisa C. Ragan

I grew up in a suburban neighborhood in a small Indiana town where almost everyone kept a garden behind their garage. We were no exception. Mom and Dad patiently tended each plant; all summer long we enjoyed fresh tomatoes, green onions, cucumbers, and bell peppers. The plant that elicited the most excitement from Mom, however, didn't come from the garden at all. A strange-looking plant with red stalks and enormous, floppy, green leaves would mysteriously sprout up every now and then in a weedy corner of our small backyard. "Rhubarb!" Mom would exclaim with delight. "Tonight I'll make a rhubarb pie."

Had she said cherry or blackberry or banana cream or just about anything else, I would have been giddy with glee. But rhubarb? First of all, it looked like red celery, and I didn't think a celery pie sounded especially tasty. Mom let me sample a bite of the rhubarb she was chopping on the kitchen counter. As soon as the

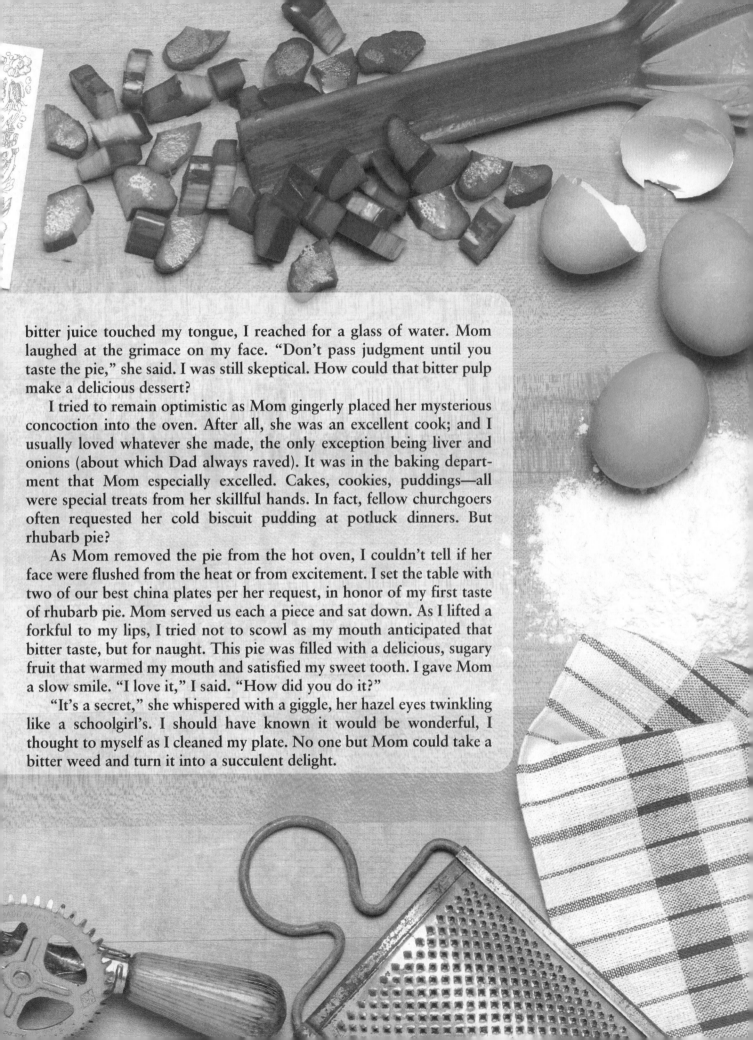

bitter juice touched my tongue, I reached for a glass of water. Mom laughed at the grimace on my face. "Don't pass judgment until you taste the pie," she said. I was still skeptical. How could that bitter pulp make a delicious dessert?

I tried to remain optimistic as Mom gingerly placed her mysterious concoction into the oven. After all, she was an excellent cook; and I usually loved whatever she made, the only exception being liver and onions (about which Dad always raved). It was in the baking department that Mom especially excelled. Cakes, cookies, puddings—all were special treats from her skillful hands. In fact, fellow churchgoers often requested her cold biscuit pudding at potluck dinners. But rhubarb pie?

As Mom removed the pie from the hot oven, I couldn't tell if her face were flushed from the heat or from excitement. I set the table with two of our best china plates per her request, in honor of my first taste of rhubarb pie. Mom served us each a piece and sat down. As I lifted a forkful to my lips, I tried not to scowl as my mouth anticipated that bitter taste, but for naught. This pie was filled with a delicious, sugary fruit that warmed my mouth and satisfied my sweet tooth. I gave Mom a slow smile. "I love it," I said. "How did you do it?"

"It's a secret," she whispered with a giggle, her hazel eyes twinkling like a schoolgirl's. I should have known it would be wonderful, I thought to myself as I cleaned my plate. No one but Mom could take a bitter weed and turn it into a succulent delight.

Bread Bait

Margaret Rorke

I telephoned to Bill and said
That I would like a loaf of bread.
He told me he would write a note
And pin it to his overcoat.

When supper time at last arrived,
I knew with someone he'd connived.
Above the sacks I saw his hat;
His arms were just as full as that.

As groc'ries filled the cupboard top,
He said, "My dear, I couldn't stop.
You know, I've never tried this cheese,
And here's the newest thing they freeze.

"This bottle looked just oh so nice,
And of this meat I bought a slice.
They say these crackers just came in,
And now they pack this stuff in tin."

The grocer has a clever trap.
He puts his foods in tempting wrap,
And on his counters they are spread
To catch the man who comes for bread.

COUNTRY KITCHEN
Jessie Walker Associates

The Country Kitchen

Anna Belle Jeffries

Gingham curtains filter sunshine;
Red tomatoes line the sill.
Baking bread and apple dumplings
With sweet smells the kitchen fill.

Yellow crocks and stoneware dishes
Sit upon the checkered cloth
With the jellies, homemade pickles,
Noodles rich in chicken broth.

Biscuits drip with golden butter;
Fresh-ground coffee perks away
On the big, old-fashioned cookstove
When we start another day.

Kitty snoozes in her basket,
Lying in a beam of sun
While we sit around the table
Waiting till the food is done.

Such a warm and cozy feeling
Fills my heart with sweet content
In my grandma's country kitchen
Where my happiest days are spent!

Legendary Americans

NANCY SKARMEAS

MARY ENGLE PENNINGTON

In the decade between 1881 and 1890, more than five million immigrants arrived on American shores looking for a better life, one peak in a wave of immigration that had begun in the middle of the nineteenth century and would continue for years to come. Most settled in the large cities of the northeast, where they joined a growing population of former rural and small town residents who had relocated to urban centers in search of work. By the turn of the twentieth century, America's large cities were dangerously overcrowded and overburdened. Along with problems of housing, employment, sanitation, public safety, and public health, city officials faced the problem of food. The issue was not finding

enough food; there were plenty of rural farmers ready to meet the demand of their neighboring cities and each day they shipped in fresh meat, eggs, and milk. The problem was that each year hundreds of American city residents died from food poisoning after eating food that had become impure from improper handling. The federal government responded to the crisis in 1906 with the Pure Food and Drug Act—aimed at improving the quality of the food on American tables—and turned to the Department of Agriculture to help implement its measures. The Department of Agriculture, in turn, called upon one of its most talented chemists, Dr. Mary Engle Pennington.

Dr. Pennington, by then in her mid-thirties, had traveled a long and difficult road to her position at the Department of Agriculture. Born in 1872 in Nashville, Tennessee, and raised in West Philadelphia, Pennsylvania, by Quaker parents, Mary announced her intention of becoming a chemist at the age of twelve. She received the loving support of her parents; but, in the years to come, few others did anything but put up barriers between Mary Pennington and her goal. At her high school, she had to lobby an incredulous administration to receive basic training in chemistry, and although she won admittance to the chemistry program at the University of Pennsylvania, when she completed her coursework, the university—reluctant to acknowledge the achievements of its female students—refused to grant her a bachelor's degree, instead issuing a "Certificate of Proficiency." Undaunted, Pennington continued as a graduate student at the university. By the time she finished her postgraduate studies in 1895, the administration relented—likely worn down by her persistence and, in spite of themselves, impressed by her talents—and granted her the doctorate in chemistry she had earned.

The hard-won degree did little, however, to impress potential employers, who uniformly resisted the idea of a female chemist. But Mary Pennington just as stubbornly refused to be discouraged; rather than lament the lack of opportunities, she simply created her own. In 1898, Pennington founded the Philadelphia Clinical Laboratory and quickly made a solid reputation for herself performing bacteriological analysis for area doctors and hospitals. Her work at the lab led to an appointment as a lecturer at the Women's Medical College of Pennsylvania and a position as head of Philadelphia's city health department bacteriological laboratory. In the latter post, Pennington toughened inspection standards for milk and worked to convince producers and transporters that it was in their best financial interest to maintain high standards of purity. Pennington's milk inspection standards were eventually put into use throughout the United States.

It was while she was employed by the city of Philadelphia that Mary Engle Pennington came to the attention of Dr. Harvey W. Wiley, the Chief of the Bureau of Chemistry at the Department of Agriculture. Dr. Wiley was studying a new method of food preservation called refrigeration, and in 1905 he asked Mary Pennington to assist him. Once again, however, Pennington, who might have assumed that she had proven herself competent beyond questions of gender, found that as a woman she faced an extra hurdle. Knowing that his supervisors would not accept the hiring of a woman chemist, Dr. Wiley had Pennington take her civil service exam as Dr. M. E. Pennington. By the time anyone discovered that M. E. was really Mary Engle Pennington, she had passed her exam and was already a proven contributor in the department. In 1908, at the age of thirty-six, Pennington became chief of the new Research Laboratory at the Department of Agriculture, with the mission of researching how refrigeration could be put to use to help meet the standards of the Pure Food and Drug Act of 1906.

In the early 1900s, refrigeration was a promising but unfulfilled concept. Mary Pennington was not the first chemist to take on the challenge of using refrigeration to improve the quality and safety of food; but she was the first to solve the problem of humidity, which had previously made refrigeration an impractical means of food preservation. Early attempts at refrigeration left food either so dry as to be inedible or so moist as to allow the growth of mold. Dr. Pennington's research pinpointed the proper level of humidity for safe and practical refrigeration. She went on to make further innovations in how food was stored, transported, packaged, and distributed. Her strength as a scientist was her ability to combine sound theory with practical applications. She advised the farmers who produced food, the shippers who transported it, the warehousers who stored it, and the grocers who sold it and made each group understand the importance of good, safe handling.

In 1919, Mary Pennington left her government job to become a consultant to private industry. She helped packing houses, storage companies, shippers, and distributors set up their organizations in a way that guaranteed freshness for all the food they handled. During World War I, Dr. Pennington served as a member of Herbert Hoover's Food Administration and received a Notable Service Medal for her innovations on refrigerated railroad cars. Dr. Pennington, devoted to science from the time she was twelve years old, never truly retired. At the time of her death in 1952, at the age of eighty, she was vice-president of the American Institution of Refrigeration.

Dr. Mary Engle Pennington faced a difficult road on the way to becoming a pioneering chemist, yet she never accepted the obstacles in her path; and her intelligence, her commitment, and her innovative accomplishments made it impossible for her peers to dismiss her on the basis of her gender. Today she should be remembered not as a woman chemist, but simply as a chemist, a scientist of great achievement whose contribution to American life cannot be underestimated. With developments in refrigeration, citizens of the nation's growing urban centers—and eventually in nearly every home from coast to coast—could rely on fresh, safe food to feed their families.

Nancy Skarmeas is a book editor and mother of a newborn son, Gordon, who is keeping her and her husband quite busy at their home in New Hampshire. Her Greek and Irish ancestry has fostered a lifelong interest in research and history.

Today

Ethel Romig Fuller

I have spread wet linen
On lavender bushes;
I have swept rose petals
From a garden walk.
I have labeled jars of raspberry jam;
I have baked a sunshine cake;
I have embroidered a yellow duck
On a small blue frock.
I have polished andirons,
Dusted the highboy,
Cut sweet peas for a black bowl,
Wound the tall clock,
Pleated a lace ruffle.
Today
I have lived a poem.

VICTORIAN PORCH
Hudson Valley Region, New York
Superstock

Home

Nellie Womack Hines

Home!
My very heart's desire is safe
Within thy walls.
The voices of my loved ones, friends who come,
My treasured books that rest in niche serene,
All make more dear to me thy haven sweet.
Nor do my feet
Desire to wander out except that they
May have the glad return at eventide,
Dear home.

Home!
My very heart's contentment lies
Within thy walls.
No worldly calls hath power to turn my eyes
In longing from thy quietness. Each morn
When I go forth upon the duties of the day,
I wend my way,
Content to know that eve will bring me
Safely to thy walls again,
Dear home.

Rendezvous

Mary Scott Fitzgerald

For just a brief while every day
I steal away from duty
And leave the indoor tasks undone
To keep a tryst with beauty.

Birdsong and lily-bell
Tinkling thin and sweet;
Sun-gold and starry bloom
Flashing at my feet;
Cool mist with crystal beads
Gleaming everywhere;
Wild plum and pink thorn
Hanging on the air.

So swiftly then I can return
To tread the rounds of duty,
Since for one fleeting breath I stood
Hand in hand with beauty.

COUNTRY GARDEN
Greenville, Indiana
Daniel Dempster Photography

From My Garden Journal

by Deana Deck

SWEET PEA

There's nothing like the hint of a familiar fragrance to take you home again. One particular fragrance takes me back in time like no other—the heavenly perfume of sweet peas. The scent floods my mind with memories of a balmy Florida spring when my dad let me help him plant a "victory garden." He placed a colorful packet of sweet-pea seeds in my grubby, four-year-old hand; then he patiently showed me how to plant and care for them. I poked them into the soil and watered them faithfully. Each day I could be found lying on my stomach in the warm, sweet-smelling dirt to search for the earliest sprouts. Later I delighted in the contraption of strings and sticks that my father and I constructed for a trellis. My patience was rewarded a thousandfold. The sweet peas grew like magic and climbed the trellis so fast you could almost see them moving. The blossoms hung gracefully from every available stem in flowing cascades of pearly pink, pale rose, and glowing magenta. Although they were beautiful to see, nothing compared to their rich, heady fragrance. The aroma wrapped itself around me and anchored itself in the heart of my sense memories for all time.

Sweet peas are not something you come across often; but when you do, you'll not soon forget them. In addition to their memorable scent, their blossoms are lovely yet fragile. But since they have short stems, you won't see sweet peas in a corsage or catch them in a bridal bouquet. A temperamental plant, sweet peas need to be carefully coaxed from their seeds by a gentle, patient gardener.

When I first moved to Tennessee, I discovered a ruined stone wall bordering a dirt road very near my home. To my delight, over the rustic wall sprawled a breathtakingly beautiful mass of sweet pea vines, all in full, deep-rose bloom. I filled vase after vase with them throughout my home. They faded, as sweet peas do, from deep pink and rose to softer mauves and lavenders as they aged; but inhale as I might, I could detect no hint of that haunting aroma I remembered so well from my childhood.

That's how I discovered that there are two types of sweet peas. One is the species I found in the alley, a reliable perennial (*Lathyrus latifolia*) that can survive in hot summer weather but lacks fragrance. The other is the annual spring flowering species (*Lathyrus oderata*) which, despite its name, also usually lacks fragrance. While hybridizers have created bigger and better sweet peas, they have neglected to preserve the plant's signature scent.

Annual sweet peas such as the ubiquitous Royal Mix are available in most garden centers and catalogs. Many catalogs extol the virtues of sweet peas by pointing out their heat resistance, larger-than-ever blooms, and a multitude of new colors. Unfortunately, most catalogs seldom mention fragrance. If you long to be enveloped in that delicate, sweet aroma on which the sweet pea's reputation was built, trust only the catalog that brags about it blatantly.

For example, a section of the Thompson and Morgan catalog is devoted to fragrant species. The catalog offers wonderful sweet peas called Antique Fantasy Mixed. Their description admits that the flowers are not the biggest available, and heat resistance isn't mentioned at all; but the words "outstanding, intoxicating fragrance" definitely got my attention.

Whatever variety of annual sweet peas you select, cultivation is the same. Sweet peas like the sun, but they can't stand heat; so plant them where they get the most morning sun you can provide but are protected in the hot afternoon. Sweet peas do well in the spring, but gardeners in warmer climates can actually plant them in the fall and enjoy them all winter.

Sweet peas demand rich, well-draining soil and do their best when planted in a trench. Dig the trench two feet wide and a foot deep; and enrich the soil with forty percent compost or manure, forty percent loam, and twenty percent sand. Fill the trench to within four inches of the surface, and place the remaining soil to one side.

Before planting, soak the seeds in tepid water for twenty-four hours; then plant them one inch deep. As the seedlings begin to grow, cover them with a half inch of soil for each two inches of growth until the trench has been filled in. When the seedlings are three or four inches tall, pinch back the central leader to encourage thicker growth and bushier plants.

The vines grow quickly, so be sure to create a support system when they are still fairly young.

A tripod of bamboo or thin branches for each plant will do. Chicken wire fencing attached to whatever you have handy provides excellent support. Strings anchored in the soil at the base of the plants and strung up a wall or fence are another easy option.

If you choose to plant perennial sweet peas, you'll need to start with container-grown plants rather than seeds since the seeds seem impossible to find. Perennial sweet peas are not as picky about their location and are quite happy out in the full sun all day. For the best results, provide them with the same rich, deep soil as the annual varieties.

Like most all varieties of sweet peas, the perennial species tends to sprawl and must have a trellis, fence, or wall to climb on. The best support is twine or wire—unless you have a stone wall in the country and do not mind the sprawl. If you yearn for sweet peas but can't provide climbing equipment for them, consider some of the newer varieties like Ferry-Morse's Jet Set Mixed, a low, spreading plant that acts more like a ground cover and requires no staking. Another option is Burpee's Pink Perfume, described as "freely flowering dwarf plants fifteen inches in height with a delightfully sweet fragrance."

As a four-year-old, I didn't go through any of the fuss of presoaking the seeds, digging out a trench, or manipulating the soil content. Today, however, that effort is necessary if you want even the slightest whiff of the long-forgotten fragrance that gave this little pea plant its name. As for me, a little effort is well worth the rewards that the perfumed aroma of the sweet pea provides— strong memories of a cherished childhood home.

Deana Deck tends to her flowers and vegetables at her home in Nashville, Tennessee, where her popular garden column is a regular feature in The Tennessean.

The Gardener

Lon Myruski

The gardener is a poet—
   He versifies his lawn
In phrases of fine flowers;
   They air a summer's song.
He has no ink, no paper;
   His pen is but a hoe,
Yet his yard speaks its beauty
   In sweet poetic flow.

The gardener is an artist—
   His skillful thumb of green
Soon culls a master still life,
   A winsome floral scene.
And who could pass his garden
   And not take notice of
Artistic stands of blossoms
   Wrought through the work he loves?

Green

Patience Strong

Green is Nature's colour.
She uses all its shades
To decorate the forests,
The gardens, and the glades.
In emerald and olive
And greens of every tone,
She dyes the wayside hedges
And tints the mossy stone.

Lovely is the mantle
O'er downs and meadows spread—
The garment of the grasses,
The bright boughs overhead.
It brings a breath of beauty
That lights up every scene—
A splash of Nature's colour,
A touch of living green.

The trees in town and city
Where brick walls block the skies
Relieve the dreary picture
And rest the weary eyes.
The green of leafy branches
Beyond the windowpanes
Reminds us of the country
And of the winding lanes.

THE SIGHTS, SMELLS, AND SOUNDS OF SUMMER

My boyhood years were spent on a northeastern hill farm with its meadows and fields, its woods and pastures, and a creek winding through the length of the farm. Farming was hard and demanding work, and I relished the fading warmth of the setting sun. I would cool off by dipping in a pool in the creek where darting minnows tickled my toes, and I often slept in a tent in the dooryard during hot summer nights. I was in love with summer, and I was home.

As a teen-ager, I loved to sleep in a tent under the moon and stars that appeared in the evening sky. My pillows were stuffed with feathers and down from our own flocks, and sleep came easily on ticks filled with straw left by the threshers.

I always left the front of the tent open so I could enjoy the fragrance of Mother's beds of four-o'clocks and the clean, refreshing aroma of dew as it sprinkled its droplets of jewels on the grass and weeds and leaves. I invited the crickets in with their mellow tremolos. Fireflies came floating through in no hurry at all to get anywhere as they flashed their blinking lights over my bed. If a mosquito flew in, its wings hummed and sang. A farm cat often came to curl up on the bed and purr itself to sleep; its purring was contentment to my ears.

In those days, lawns were not groomed every week as they are now. Our yard would go weeks without tending, and grass and clover and weeds thrived around the tent. Dandelions wore their golden bonnets, chickweed its starlike gems.

There was music in the night—the chirping of the crickets, bullfrogs thumping their drums in the swamp with its alders and reeds and cattails, its arums and lilies. Sometimes the eerie screech of the owl would break the quietness, or a fox would yelp from the pasture across the creek.

On rainy nights, I found comfort in the rhythmic pattering of the rain. At times, the roaring rumbles and booms of a thundershower sent its jagged streaks of lightning to illuminate in a flash the darkened world around me.

Sometimes I wish I could take to the tent again for some soft summer nights under the stars. I could, I suppose, go on a camping trip somewhere; but it wouldn't be the same without my boyhood home. Nor would it be the same without the boy himself. So tonight I will let my dreams take me back to long-ago years when I exchanged my upstairs bedroom for a tent in summer's backyard.

The author of two published books, Lansing Christman has been contributing to Ideals *for more than twenty years. Mr. Christman has also been published in several American, foreign, and braille anthologies. He lives in rural South Carolina.*

Sounds of Peace

Edna Jaques

I love the sounds of peace about my ears,
The slow and steady ticking of a clock,
A quiet river running to the sea,
The homey chatter of a farmyard flock.

The whirr of quiet wings above the roof,
An old cow slowly chewing on her cud,
A flock of sheep beneath a maple tree,
An apple falling with a little thud.

I love the sound of people in a church,
The choir coming in in cap and gown,
The old bell ringing in its ivied tower,
Sending its echoes half across the town.

The sound of oars somewhere beyond the mist
As early fishermen put out to sea,
The creak of branches in the dead of night
As a small wind goes by and rocks a tree.

The crackle of a fire in the grate,
A kettle on the stove that softly sings,
I am so glad that I have ears to hear
The little muted sounds of quiet things.

Readers' Forum

Meet Our Ideals Readers and Their Families

ATTENTION *IDEALS* READERS: The *Ideals* editors want your "favorite memories" to share in an upcoming issue of *Ideals*. Do you have a special memory of a holiday shared with family or friends? Send your story of about 200 typed words to: Favorite Memories, c/o Editorial Department, Ideals Publications Inc., P.O. Box 305300, Nashville, Tennessee 37230. *Manuscripts cannot be returned.*

From WILLIAM KNIERIM of East Dubuque, Illinois, comes this adorable photograph of grandson and notorious "chow hound" Eric William Knierim, who is definitely not a finicky eater. The picture was snapped by William's wife Adele while the couple were visiting Eric and his parents, Eric and Diane Knierim, on Long Island, New York.

Austin Ellefson happily waters Grandpa's flowers in this picture sent to us by grandmother CAROL ELLEFSON of Buffalo, Minnesota. She tells us that Austin is only one of her five grandchildren, all of whom love to visit her and play in the spacious backyard. Carol and husband Don Ellefson have been married for forty-six years, and they love to keep their home lively with the precious laughter of their grandchildren. The Ellefsons have been subscribers to *Ideals* for over twenty years and are delighted to share it with their family and friends.

Ashley Marie Campbell, ten months old, sere-
nades us in this photograph sent by her grandmother, BETH MAY of Greensboro, North Carolina. Ashley and her father often "jazz it up"
together, says Mrs. May, and Ashley doesn't even
need to look at the music! Ashley lives with her
parents, Gordon and Kim Campbell, in Winston-
Salem, North Carolina, just twenty miles away
from Grandma and Grandpa's house.

Thank you William Knierim,
Carol Ellefson, and Beth May for
sharing with *Ideals*. We hope to
hear from other readers who
would like to share photos and
stories with the *Ideals* family.
Please include a self-addressed,
stamped envelope if you would
like the photos returned. Keep
your original photographs for
safekeeping and send duplicate
photos along with your name,
address, and telephone number to:

READERS' FORUM
IDEALS PUBLICATIONS INC.
P.O. BOX 305300
NASHVILLE, TENNESSEE 37230

ideals®

Publisher, Patricia A. Pingry
Editor, Lisa C. Ragan
Copy Editor, Michelle Prater Burke
Designer, Anne Lesemann
Editorial Assistant, Brian L. Bacon
Editorial Intern, Lara Davies
Contributing Editors,
Lansing Christman, Deana Deck, Russ Flint,
Pamela Kennedy, Patrick McRae, Mary
Skarmeas, Nancy Skarmeas

ACKNOWLEDGMENTS

HOME AND CHILDREN from *LIVING THE YEARS* by
Edgar A. Guest, copyright ©1949 by The Reilly & Lee Co.
Used by permission of the author's estate. DESIGN FOR
LIVING and SOUNDS OF PEACE from *THE GOLDEN
ROAD* by Edna Jaques, copyright ©1953 by Thomas
Allen & Son, Limited. Used by permission. BUYING A
FARM from *NEW ENGLAND HERITAGE AND OTHER
POEMS* by Rose Koralewsky, copyright ©1949 by Bruce
Humphries, Inc. Reprinted courtesy of Branden Publishing
Company, Boston. SONG FOR A LITTLE HOUSE by
Christopher Morley, copyright ©1921, 1949 by Christo-
pher Morley. Reprinted by permission of HarperCollins
Publishers. GREEN from *THE WINDING ROAD* by
Patience Strong, copyright ©1957 by Patience Strong.
Reprinted by permission of Rupert Crew Limited. Our sin-
cere thanks to the following authors whom we were
unable to contact: Mary Scott Fitzgerald for REN-
DEZVOUS, Ethel Romig Fuller for TODAY, Nellie Wom-
ack Hines for HOME, Donna R. Lydston for THE FAMILY,
and Catherine Parmenter Newell for DREAM HOUSE.

Summer's End

Louise Weibert Sutton

Now summer fields are white with Queen Anne's lace;
Soon fruit, matured, will bend the apple's bough.
Barefooted through the dust small children race,
Contented with the joys of here and now.
Attesting to a breeze that sighs along,
Warm clover nods, bee-kissed in noonday sun;
And at the rasp of brown cicadas' song,
I find myself with drowsy nature, one.
Too soon will ample August take her leave
And from these grassy hills of peace depart;
Too soon the yellow spider's lacy weave
Will be forgotten, and the meadowlark.
But let the coming Winter have his way;
Some gold must linger from this perfect day!

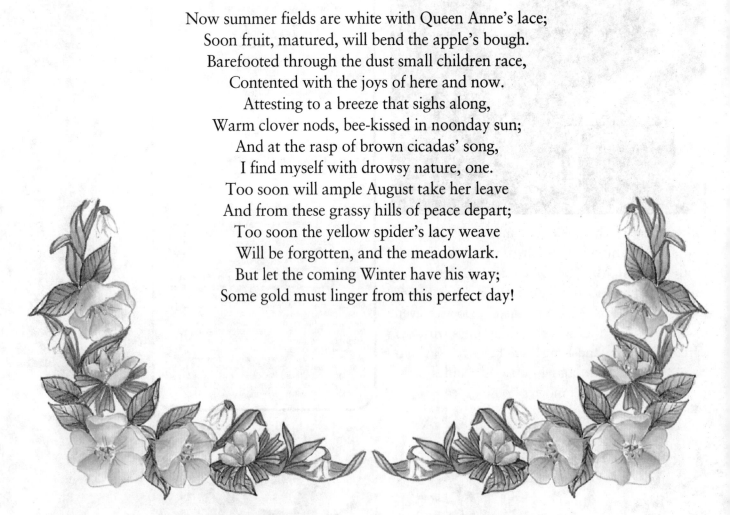

Recapture times past in the pages of . . .
REMEMBER WHEN

♦ *160 PAGES*
♦ *8 CHAPTERS*
♦ *OVER 80 MAGNIFICENT PHOTOS!*

This nostalgic look back at the life and times of half-forgotten yesteryears includes wonderful photos of bygone days in small town America . . . songs and music like "Shine On Harvest Moon" . . . evocative poems and prose to rekindle the spirit of times past—160 heartwarming, beautifully illustrated pages to delight you, year after year. Order your copy today and be sure to add extra copies to your order as gifts for friends and family!

Eight moving chapters remind us of the old-fashioned things that still live in our hearts . . .

Chapter One: Journey Home . . . Filled to the brim with that deliciously familiar "coming home" feeling.

Chapter Two: Memories of Family . . . This chapter celebrates the warmth of close moments with family members, beginning with Mom and Dad.

Chapter Three: Scrapbook of Friends . . . Some of our best memories are of the company we kept during our formative years.

Chapter Four: Recollections of the Neighborhood . . . Most of us grew up in a neighborhood that was a lot like a village—even if it was part of a big city.

Chapter Five: Remembrances of Hometown . . . Small-town America is often the best place to search for the past.

Chapter Six: Souvenirs of Trips . . . To the strains of "In My Merry Oldsmobile," relive memories of summer vacations and trips to Grandma's house.

Chapter Seven: Mementoes from First Loves . . . This chapter may bring a tear to your eye with visions of a pressed corsage and dancing to the music of an antique Victrola.

Chapter Eight: Traditions of Holidays . . . Holiday memories deserve a special place in any remembrance of times past.

Wonderful photos, delightful songs, and evocative poems and prose rekindle the spirit of times past!

Remember When offers so much to capture your fancy and take you back through the years to gentler times when America seemed younger, more innocent than today. Use your Free Examination Certificate to order a copy for yourself— and extras as gifts for friends. Then set aside a quiet evening to explore it at your leisure. It's yours for

30 DAYS FREE!

MAIL TODAY TO: Ideals Publications Inc. PO Box 305300, Nashville, TN 37230

FREE EXAMINATION CERTIFICATE

❏ **YES!** I'd like to examine *Remember When* for 30 days free. If after a month I am not delighted with it, I may return it and owe nothing. If I decide to keep it, I will be billed $19.95 plus shipping and handling. In either case, the FREE Mystery Gift is mine to keep.
Please print your name and address:

MY NAME _____

MY ADDRESS _____

CITY _____ STATE ZIP
Do you wish a copy for yourself? ❏ Yes ❏ No   For gift copies complete below:

Gift Name _____   Gift Name _____

Address _____   Address _____

City _____ State __ ZIP _____   City _____ State __ ZIP _____

❏ Please Bill Me   ❏ Charge My: ❏ MasterCard   ❏ Visa   ❏ Diners   ❏ Discover

Expiration Date: _____

Signature _____

Orders subject to acceptance. We regret that we cannot process orders from outside the U.S.   BC 000

If you believe there's a lesson to be learned from exploring the past, from allowing ourselves to be reminded of how things were a long time ago, in what children used to call "the olden days," you'll be glad *Ideals* decided to publish

REMEMBER WHEN

Summertime. After-dinner family evenings on the porch. No air conditioners. Maybe a glass of iced tea or a window fan to ease the heat. "Alexander's Ragtime Band" on the Victor Talking Machine. And a cheery wave from the minister as he chugs by in his Model A. Those were the days. Bring them back to friends and family with this very special gift idea from *Ideals*. Let them enjoy 160 beautifully illustrated pages that stir nostalgic memories of those bygone days of innocence in America . . .

INCLUDES FREE Mystery Gift!

Lots and lots of wonderful photos of life in days gone by . . . Some are full-color photos. Some are black and white. Some are photos that were originally black and white but that were hand-tinted in color before the days of color photography. All of them display heart-warming scenes from America's past—street scenes of the small home towns and big cities of yes-teryear . . . stunning "still life" photo compositions of the magazines, toys, food cartons, and artifacts that were part of everyday life back then . . . ornate postcards telling of long-forgotten travels and family vacations . . . valentine cards and greeting cards from long-ago seasons and much more!

Delightful songs and music to bring back the feeling of vanished decades . . . Perhaps there's nothing quite like a song or a piece of music to take us back to times past. Just the thought of a voice humming "Take Me Out to the Ball Game" or "Shine On Harvest Moon" is enough to make us think of turn-of-the-century lasses in wasp-waisted dresses laughing with gentlemen in spats and cravats. You'll find lots of songs and nostalgic music in *Remember When*—in fact, every chapter begins with a carefully chosen musical selection!

Evocative poems and thought-provoking prose to rekindle the spirit of times past . . . *Remember When* is certainly a book to look at. It's also very much a book to read. Ideals' editors sifted through literally thousands of possible selections of prose and poetry to choose the ones that most vividly recalled the thoughts and feelings of bygone days. You'll find plenty of delightful reading to fill many a warm, happy evening during your 30 DAY FREE EXAMINATION!

Journey Home . . . Memories of Family . . . Scrapbooks of Friends . . . Recollections of the Neighborhood . . . Remembrances of Hometown . . . Souvenirs of Trips . . . Mementoes from First Loves . . . Traditions of Holidays

COMPLETE THE FORM ON THE REVERSE SIDE NOW TO ORDER *REMEMBER WHEN* FOR 30 DAYS FREE!